This Fishing Log
Belongs To:

_____

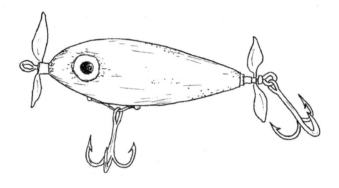

Using This Log:

- Record the date, time and location (including the GPS coordinates, if you are using them) on the blanks at the top of each page.

- To record the lunar phase, simply draw a quick outline of the current moon phase and check either waxing or waning. If the moon is currently getting larger it is "waxing", and if it is shrinking it is "waning".

- For "Wind & Weather" you can record as little or as much information as you like. Examples include temperature, wind speed, rain, sun, clouds or even the barometric pressure and humidity.

- On the second page of each log entry is a place to paste a photo or draw a sketch of something from that day's fishing trip. It can be a fish, or anything you found interesting or memorable.

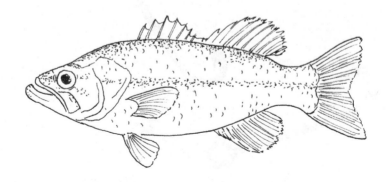

The Palomar Knot

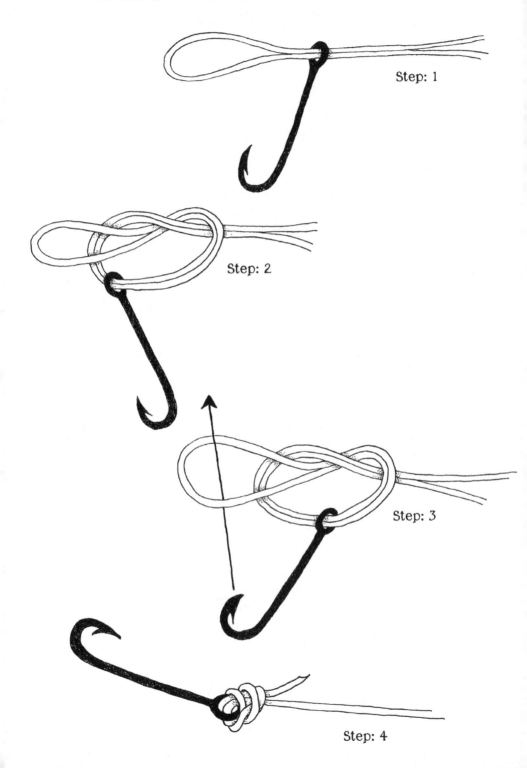

Step: 1

Step: 2

Step: 3

Step: 4

Improved Clinch Knot

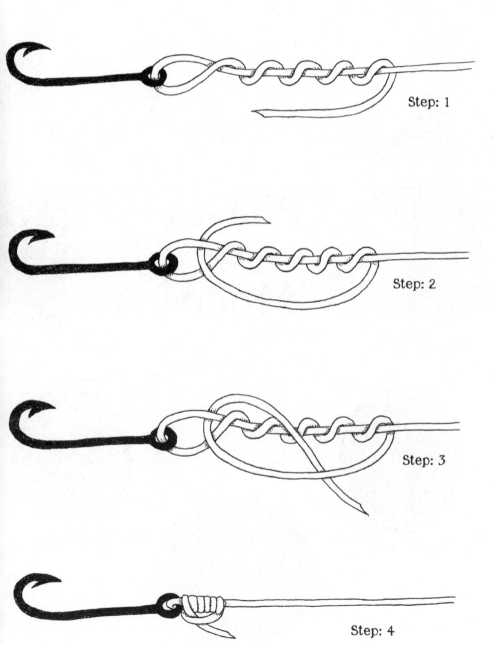

Step: 1

Step: 2

Step: 3

Step: 4

Full Moon

Waxing Gibbous

Waning Gibbous

Phases *of the* Moon

Waxing Quarter

Waning Quarter

Waxing Crescent

Waning Crescent

New Moon

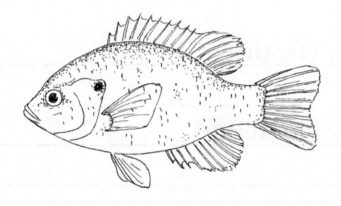

Date:	Lunar Phase
Time:	
Location:	
	○ Waxing
	○ Waning

Wind & Weather:

Lures / Bait Used:

Total Catch:

Species Caught:

Size of Smallest:

Size of Largest:

Notes:

A Photo or Sketch From This Fishing Trip

More Notes:

_____

_____

_____

_____

_____

_____

_____

_____

_____

Date:	Lunar Phase
Time:	
Location:	
	○ Waxing
	○ Waning

Wind & Weather:

Lures / Bait Used:

Total Catch:

Species Caught:

Size of Smallest:

Size of Largest:

Notes:

A Photo or Sketch From This Fishing Trip

More Notes:
_____
_____
_____
_____
_____
_____
_____
_____
_____
_____

Date:	Lunar Phase
Time:	
Location:	
	○ Waxing
	○ Waning

Wind & Weather:

Lures / Bait Used:

Total Catch:

Species Caught:

Size of Smallest:

Size of Largest:

Notes:

A Photo or Sketch From This Fishing Trip

More Notes:

_____

_____

_____

_____

_____

_____

_____

_____

_____

Date:	Lunar Phase
Time:	
Location:	
	○ Waxing
	○ Waning

Wind & Weather:

Lures / Bait Used:

Total Catch:

Species Caught:

Size of Smallest:

Size of Largest:

Notes:

A Photo or Sketch From This Fishing Trip

More Notes:

Date:	Lunar Phase
Time:	
Location:	
	○ Waxing
	○ Waning

Wind & Weather:

Lures / Bait Used:

Total Catch:

Species Caught:

Size of Smallest:

Size of Largest:

Notes:

A Photo or Sketch From This Fishing Trip

lore Notes:

Date:	Lunar Phase
Time:	
Location:	
	○ Waxing
	○ Waning

Wind & Weather:

_____

Lures / Bait Used:

_____

Total Catch:

Species Caught:

_____

Size of Smallest:

Size of Largest:

Notes:

_____

_____

_____

_____

_____

A Photo or Sketch From This Fishing Trip

More Notes:
_____
_____
_____
_____
_____
_____
_____
_____
_____

Date:	Lunar Phase
Time:	
Location:	
	○ Waxing
	○ Waning

Wind & Weather:

Lures / Bait Used:

Total Catch:

Species Caught:

Size of Smallest:

Size of Largest:

Notes:

A Photo or Sketch From This Fishing Trip

More Notes:

Date:	Lunar Phase
Time:	
Location:	
	○ Waxing
	○ Waning

Wind & Weather:

Lures / Bait Used:

Total Catch:

Species Caught:

Size of Smallest:

Size of Largest:

Notes:

A Photo or Sketch From This Fishing Trip

More Notes:

_____
_____
_____
_____
_____
_____
_____
_____
_____
_____
_____

Date:	Lunar Phase
Time:	
Location:	
	○ Waxing
	○ Waning

Wind & Weather:

_____

Lures / Bait Used:

_____

Total Catch:

Species Caught:

_____

Size of Smallest:

Size of Largest:

Notes:

_____

_____

_____

_____

A Photo or Sketch From This Fishing Trip

More Notes:

_____
_____
_____
_____
_____
_____
_____
_____
_____

Date:	Lunar Phase
Time:	
Location:	
	○ Waxing
	○ Waning

Wind & Weather:

Lures / Bait Used:

Total Catch:

Species Caught:

Size of Smallest:

Size of Largest:

Notes:

A Photo or Sketch From This Fishing Trip

More Notes:

Date:	Lunar Phase
Time:	
Location:	
	○ Waxing
	○ Waning

Wind & Weather:

Lures / Bait Used:

Total Catch:

Species Caught:

Size of Smallest:

Size of Largest:

Notes:

A Photo or Sketch From This Fishing Trip

ore Notes:

Date:	Lunar Phase
Time:	
Location:	
	◯ Waxing
	◯ Waning

Wind & Weather:

Lures / Bait Used:

Total Catch:

Species Caught:

Size of Smallest:

Size of Largest:

Notes:

A Photo or Sketch From This Fishing Trip

More Notes:

Date:	Lunar Phase
Time:	
Location:	
	○ Waxing
	○ Waning

Wind & Weather:

Lures / Bait Used:

Total Catch:

Species Caught:

Size of Smallest:

Size of Largest:

Notes:

A Photo or Sketch From This Fishing Trip

More Notes:
_____
_____
_____
_____
_____
_____
_____
_____
_____
_____

Date:	Lunar Phase
Time:	
Location:	
	○ Waxing
	○ Waning

Wind & Weather:

Lures / Bait Used:

Total Catch:

Species Caught:

Size of Smallest:

Size of Largest:

Notes:

A Photo or Sketch From This Fishing Trip

More Notes:

Date:	Lunar Phase
Time:	
Location:	
	○ Waxing
	○ Waning

Wind & Weather:

_____

Lures / Bait Used:

_____

Total Catch:

Species Caught:

_____

Size of Smallest:

Size of Largest:

Notes:

_____

_____

_____

_____

_____

A Photo or Sketch From This Fishing Trip

More Notes:
_____
_____
_____
_____
_____
_____
_____
_____
_____
_____

Date:	Lunar Phase
Time:	
Location:	
	○ Waxing
	○ Waning

Wind & Weather:

Lures / Bait Used:

Total Catch:

Species Caught:

Size of Smallest:

Size of Largest:

Notes:

A Photo or Sketch From This Fishing Trip

More Notes:

_____

_____

_____

_____

_____

_____

_____

_____

_____

_____

Date:	Lunar Phase
Time:	
Location:	
	○ Waxing
	○ Waning

Wind & Weather:

Lures / Bait Used:

Total Catch:

Species Caught:

Size of Smallest:

Size of Largest:

Notes:

A Photo or Sketch From This Fishing Trip

More Notes:

_____
_____
_____
_____
_____
_____
_____
_____
_____

Date:	Lunar Phase
Time:	
Location:	
	○ Waxing
	○ Waning

Wind & Weather:

Lures / Bait Used:

Total Catch:

Species Caught:

Size of Smallest:

Size of Largest:

Notes:

A Photo or Sketch From This Fishing Trip

More Notes:

Date:	Lunar Phase
Time:	
Location:	
	○ Waxing
	○ Waning

Wind & Weather:

Lures / Bait Used:

Total Catch:

Species Caught:

Size of Smallest:

Size of Largest:

Notes:

A Photo or Sketch From This Fishing Trip

More Notes:

_____

_____

_____

_____

_____

_____

_____

_____

_____

Date:	Lunar Phase
Time:	
Location:	
	○ Waxing
	○ Waning

Wind & Weather:

Lures / Bait Used:

Total Catch:

Species Caught:

Size of Smallest:

Size of Largest:

Notes:

A Photo or Sketch From This Fishing Trip

More Notes:

Date:	Lunar Phase
Time:	
Location:	
	○ Waxing
	○ Waning

Wind & Weather:

Lures / Bait Used:

Total Catch:

Species Caught:

Size of Smallest:

Size of Largest:

Notes:

A Photo or Sketch From This Fishing Trip

More Notes:

_____

_____

_____

_____

_____

_____

_____

_____

_____

_____

Date:	Lunar Phase
Time:	
Location:	
	○ Waxing
	○ Waning

Wind & Weather:

Lures / Bait Used:

Total Catch:

Species Caught:

Size of Smallest:

Size of Largest:

Notes:

A Photo or Sketch From This Fishing Trip

More Notes:
_____
_____
_____
_____
_____
_____
_____
_____
_____

Date:	Lunar Phase
Time:	
Location:	
	○ Waxing
	○ Waning

Wind & Weather:

Lures / Bait Used:

Total Catch:

Species Caught:

Size of Smallest:

Size of Largest:

Notes:

A Photo or Sketch From This Fishing Trip

lore Notes:

_____

_____

_____

_____

_____

_____

_____

_____

_____

Date:	Lunar Phase
Time:	
Location:	
	○ Waxing
	○ Waning

Wind & Weather:

Lures / Bait Used:

Total Catch:

Species Caught:

Size of Smallest:

Size of Largest:

Notes:

A Photo or Sketch From This Fishing Trip

More Notes:
_____
_____
_____
_____
_____
_____
_____
_____
_____

Date:	Lunar Phase
Time:	
Location:	
	○ Waxing
	○ Waning

Wind & Weather:

Lures / Bait Used:

Total Catch:

Species Caught:

Size of Smallest:

Size of Largest:

Notes:

A Photo or Sketch From This Fishing Trip

More Notes:

Date:	Lunar Phase
Time:	
Location:	
	○ Waxing
	○ Waning

Wind & Weather:

Lures / Bait Used:

Total Catch:

Species Caught:

Size of Smallest:

Size of Largest:

Notes:

More Notes:

Date:	Lunar Phase
Time:	
Location:	
	○ Waxing
	○ Waning

Wind & Weather:

Lures / Bait Used:

Total Catch:

Species Caught:

Size of Smallest:

Size of Largest:

Notes:

A Photo or Sketch From This Fishing Trip

More Notes:

Date:	Lunar Phase
Time:	
Location:	
	○ Waxing
	○ Waning

Wind & Weather:

Lures / Bait Used:

Total Catch:

Species Caught:

Size of Smallest:

Size of Largest:

Notes:

A Photo or Sketch From This Fishing Trip

More Notes:

Date:	Lunar Phase
Time:	
Location:	
	○ Waxing
	○ Waning

Wind & Weather:

Lures / Bait Used:

Total Catch:

Species Caught:

Size of Smallest:

Size of Largest:

Notes:

A Photo or Sketch From This Fishing Trip

More Notes:

Date:	Lunar Phase
Time:	
Location:	
	○ Waxing
	○ Waning

Wind & Weather:

Lures / Bait Used:

Total Catch:

Species Caught:

Size of Smallest:

Size of Largest:

Notes:

A Photo or Sketch From This Fishing Trip

More Notes:
_____
_____
_____
_____
_____
_____
_____
_____
_____
_____

Date:	Lunar Phase
Time:	
Location:	
	○ Waxing
	○ Waning

Wind & Weather:

Lures / Bait Used:

Total Catch:

Species Caught:

Size of Smallest:

Size of Largest:

Notes:

A Photo or Sketch From This Fishing Trip

More Notes:

Date:	Lunar Phase
Time:	
Location:	
	○ Waxing
	○ Waning

Wind & Weather:

Lures / Bait Used:

Total Catch:

Species Caught:

Size of Smallest:

Size of Largest:

Notes:

A Photo or Sketch From This Fishing Trip

lore Notes:

_____

_____

_____

_____

_____

_____

_____

_____

_____

Date:

Time:

Location:

Lunar Phase

○ Waxing
○ Waning

Wind & Weather:

Lures / Bait Used:

Total Catch:

Species Caught:

Size of Smallest:

Size of Largest:

Notes:

A Photo or Sketch From This Fishing Trip

More Notes:

_____

_____

_____

_____

_____

_____

_____

_____

_____

_____

Date:	Lunar Phase
Time:	
Location:	
	○ Waxing
	○ Waning

Wind & Weather:

Lures / Bait Used:

Total Catch:

Species Caught:

Size of Smallest:

Size of Largest:

Notes:

A Photo or Sketch From This Fishing Trip

More Notes:

Date:	Lunar Phase
Time:	
Location:	
	○ Waxing
	○ Waning

Wind & Weather:

Lures / Bait Used:

Total Catch:

Species Caught:

Size of Smallest:

Size of Largest:

Notes:

A Photo or Sketch From This Fishing Trip

More Notes:

Date:	Lunar Phase
Time:	
Location:	
	○ Waxing
	○ Waning

Wind & Weather:

Lures / Bait Used:

Total Catch:

Species Caught:

Size of Smallest:

Size of Largest:

Notes:

A Photo or Sketch From This Fishing Trip

More Notes:

Date:	Lunar Phase
Time:	
Location:	
	○ Waxing
	○ Waning

Wind & Weather:

Lures / Bait Used:

Total Catch:

Species Caught:

Size of Smallest:

Size of Largest:

Notes:

A Photo or Sketch From This Fishing Trip

More Notes:

Date:	Lunar Phase
Time:	
Location:	
	○ Waxing
	○ Waning

Wind & Weather:

Lures / Bait Used:

Total Catch:

Species Caught:

Size of Smallest:

Size of Largest:

Notes:

A Photo or Sketch From This Fishing Trip

More Notes:

Date:	Lunar Phase
Time:	
Location:	
	○ Waxing
	○ Waning

Wind & Weather:

Lures / Bait Used:

Total Catch:

Species Caught:

Size of Smallest:

Size of Largest:

Notes:

A Photo or Sketch From This Fishing Trip

More Notes:

Date:	Lunar Phase
Time:	
Location:	
	○ Waxing
	○ Waning

Wind & Weather:

Lures / Bait Used:

Total Catch:

Species Caught:

Size of Smallest:

Size of Largest:

Notes:

A Photo or Sketch From This Fishing Trip

More Notes:

_____

_____

_____

_____

_____

_____

_____

_____

_____

_____

Date:	Lunar Phase
Time:	
Location:	
	○ Waxing
	○ Waning

Wind & Weather:

Lures / Bait Used:

Total Catch:

Species Caught:

Size of Smallest:

Size of Largest:

Notes:

A Photo or Sketch From This Fishing Trip

More Notes:

_____

_____

_____

_____

_____

_____

_____

_____

_____

Date:	Lunar Phase
Time:	
Location:	
	○ Waxing
	○ Waning

Wind & Weather:

Lures / Bait Used:

Total Catch:

Species Caught:

Size of Smallest:

Size of Largest:

Notes:

A Photo or Sketch From This Fishing Trip

More Notes:

_____
_____
_____
_____
_____
_____
_____
_____
_____
_____
_____
_____

Date:	Lunar Phase
Time:	
Location:	
	○ Waxing
	○ Waning

Wind & Weather:

Lures / Bait Used:

Total Catch:

Species Caught:

Size of Smallest:

Size of Largest:

Notes:

A Photo or Sketch From This Fishing Trip

More Notes:
_____
_____
_____
_____
_____
_____
_____
_____
_____
_____

Date:	Lunar Phase
Time:	
Location:	
	○ Waxing
	○ Waning

Wind & Weather:

Lures / Bait Used:

Total Catch:

Species Caught:

Size of Smallest:

Size of Largest:

Notes:

A Photo or Sketch From This Fishing Trip

More Notes:

_____

_____

_____

_____

_____

_____

_____

_____

_____

_____

Date:	Lunar Phase
Time:	
Location:	
	○ Waxing
	○ Waning

Wind & Weather:

Lures / Bait Used:

Total Catch:

Species Caught:

Size of Smallest:

Size of Largest:

Notes:

A Photo or Sketch From This Fishing Trip

More Notes:

_____
_____
_____
_____
_____
_____
_____
_____
_____

Date:	Lunar Phase
Time:	
Location:	
	○ Waxing
	○ Waning

Wind & Weather:

Lures / Bait Used:

Total Catch:

Species Caught:

Size of Smallest:

Size of Largest:

Notes:

A Photo or Sketch From This Fishing Trip

More Notes:
_____
_____
_____
_____
_____
_____
_____
_____
_____
_____
_____
_____

Date:	Lunar Phase
Time:	
Location:	
	○ Waxing
	○ Waning

Wind & Weather:

Lures / Bait Used:

Total Catch:

Species Caught:

Size of Smallest:

Size of Largest:

Notes:

A Photo or Sketch From This Fishing Trip

ore Notes:

_____

_____

_____

_____

_____

_____

_____

_____

_____

_____

Date:	Lunar Phase
Time:	
Location:	
	○ Waxing
	○ Waning

Wind & Weather:

Lures / Bait Used:

Total Catch:

Species Caught:

Size of Smallest:

Size of Largest:

Notes:

A Photo or Sketch From This Fishing Trip

More Notes:
_____
_____
_____
_____
_____
_____
_____
_____
_____

Date:	Lunar Phase
Time:	
Location:	
	○ Waxing
	○ Waning

Wind & Weather:

Lures / Bait Used:

Total Catch:

Species Caught:

Size of Smallest:

Size of Largest:

Notes:

A Photo or Sketch From This Fishing Trip

More Notes:
_____
_____
_____
_____
_____
_____
_____
_____
_____

Date:	Lunar Phase
Time:	
Location:	
	○ Waxing
	○ Waning

Wind & Weather:

Lures / Bait Used:

Total Catch:

Species Caught:

Size of Smallest:

Size of Largest:

Notes:

A Photo or Sketch From This Fishing Trip

More Notes:

_____

_____

_____

_____

_____

_____

_____

_____

_____

_____

_____

_____

Date:	Lunar Phase
Time:	
Location:	
	○ Waxing
	○ Waning

Wind & Weather:

Lures / Bait Used:

Total Catch:

Species Caught:

Size of Smallest:

Size of Largest:

Notes:

A Photo or Sketch From This Fishing Trip

More Notes:

_____

_____

_____

_____

_____

_____

_____

_____

_____

_____

"Many men go fishing all of their lives without knowing that it is not fish they are after."

~ *Henry David Thoreau*

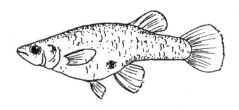

Made in the USA
Coppell, TX
23 May 2021